D0462927

HORSES

SEYMOUR SIMON

Updated Edition

HARPER
An Imprint of HarperCollinsPublishers

To Liz Nealon, my wife and helpmate

Special thanks to Robert Byrne

HarperCollins
PUBLISHERS
Since 1817

PHOTO CREDITS:

Page 2: © Gigja Einarsdottir/Getty Images; page 4: © Gigja Einarsdottir/Getty Images; page 5: © Philippe Psaila/Science Source; page 7: © H. Zell; pages 8-9: © John Shaw/Science Source; page 11: © smereka/Shutterstock; page 12: © Studio 37/Shutterstock; pages 14-15: © Frans Lanting/MINT Images/Science Source; page 16: © AsyaPozniak/Shutterstock; pages 18-19: © Rolf Kopfle/Science Source; page 20: © Elisabeth Weiland/Science Source; pages 22-23: © Hans D. Dossenbach/Science Source; page 25: © Olga_i / Shutterstock; page 26: © Roger Wilmshurst/Science Source; page 29: © Jean-Michel Labat/Science Source; page 30: © Mauro Fermariello/Science Source

Horses

Copyright © 2006, 2017 by Seymour Simon
All rights reserved. Manufactured in China.
No part of this book may be used or reproduced in any manner whatsoever without written permission except in the case of brief quotations embodied in critical articles and reviews. For information address HarperCollins Children's Books, a division of HarperCollins Publishers, 195 Broadway, New York, NY 10007.
www.harpercollinschildrens.com

ISBN 978-0-06-237439-4 (trade bdg.) — ISBN 978-0-06-446256-3 (pbk.)

17   18   19   20   21   SCP   10   9   8   7   6   5   4   3   2   1

❖

Revised edition, 2017

Author's Note

From a young age, I was interested in animals, space, my surroundings—all the natural sciences. When I was a teenager, I became the president of a nationwide junior astronomy club with a thousand members. After college, I became a classroom teacher for nearly twenty-five years while also writing articles and books for children on science and nature even before I became a full-time writer. My experience as a teacher gives me the ability to understand how to reach my young readers and get them interested in the world around us.

I've written more than 300 books, and I've thought a lot about different ways to encourage interest in the natural world, as well as how to show the joys of nonfiction. When I write, I use comparisons to help explain unfamiliar ideas, complex concepts, and impossibly large numbers. I try to engage your senses and imagination to set the scene and to make science fun. For example, in *Penguins*, I emphasize the playful nature of these creatures on the very first page by mentioning how penguins excel at swimming and diving. I use strong verbs to enhance understanding. I make use of descriptive detail and ask questions that anticipate what you may be thinking (sometimes right at the start of the book).

Many of my books are photo-essays, which use extraordinary photographs to amplify and expand the text, creating different and engaging ways of exploring nonfiction. You'll also find a glossary, an index, and website and research recommendations in most of my books, which make them ideal for enhancing your reading and learning experience. As William Blake wrote in his poem, I want my readers "to see a world in a grain of sand, / And a heaven in a wild flower, / Hold infinity in the palm of your hand, / And eternity in an hour."

Seymour Simon

Horses have always been very much a part of human life. During the last Ice Age, tens of thousands of years ago, people made cave drawings of horses. Today people create movies and books about horses.

More than five thousand years ago, early peoples tamed and herded horses on the grassy plains of Europe and Asia. During the ancient Babylonian, Greek, and Roman civilizations, people trained horses to draw their war chariots. Genghis Khan conquered Asia and eastern Europe with an army of a quarter of a million horsemen. Horses carried medieval knights and their armor into battle. The cowboys, the Native Americans of the western plains, and their horses were an important part of American history.

The ancestor of the horse, *Hyracotherium*, which means "mole beast," lived about fifty-five million years ago in the forests of what is now Europe and eastern Asia. It looked only slightly like the horses we know today. It was about the size of a spaniel and ate the leaves of trees. This small horse is also called *Eohippus*, which means "dawn horse."

Over tens of millions of years, horses slowly changed. *Mesohippus*, which means "middle horse," was the size of a large dog, about two feet high. It ate both tree leaves and grasses.

About ten million years ago, the first single-toed, or single-**hoofed**, horse roamed the plains of Europe and Asia. It was about as big as a pony and ate only grasses. *Equus*, the modern-day horse, appeared about two million years ago and is now found over much of the world.

Equus
Recent

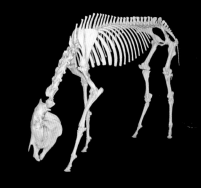 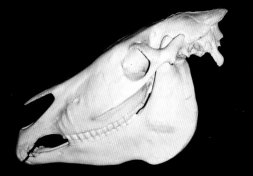 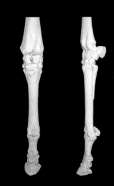

Pliohippus
Late Miocene

  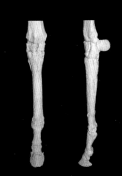

Merychippus
Middle Miocene

  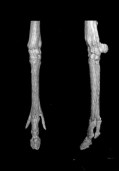

Mesohippus
Late Eocene

  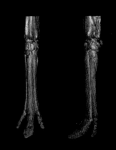

Around five hundred years ago, horses were brought to America by Spanish explorers. The Europeans used their horses to help battle the Native Americans and for trading purposes. Some horses escaped and lived in the wild.

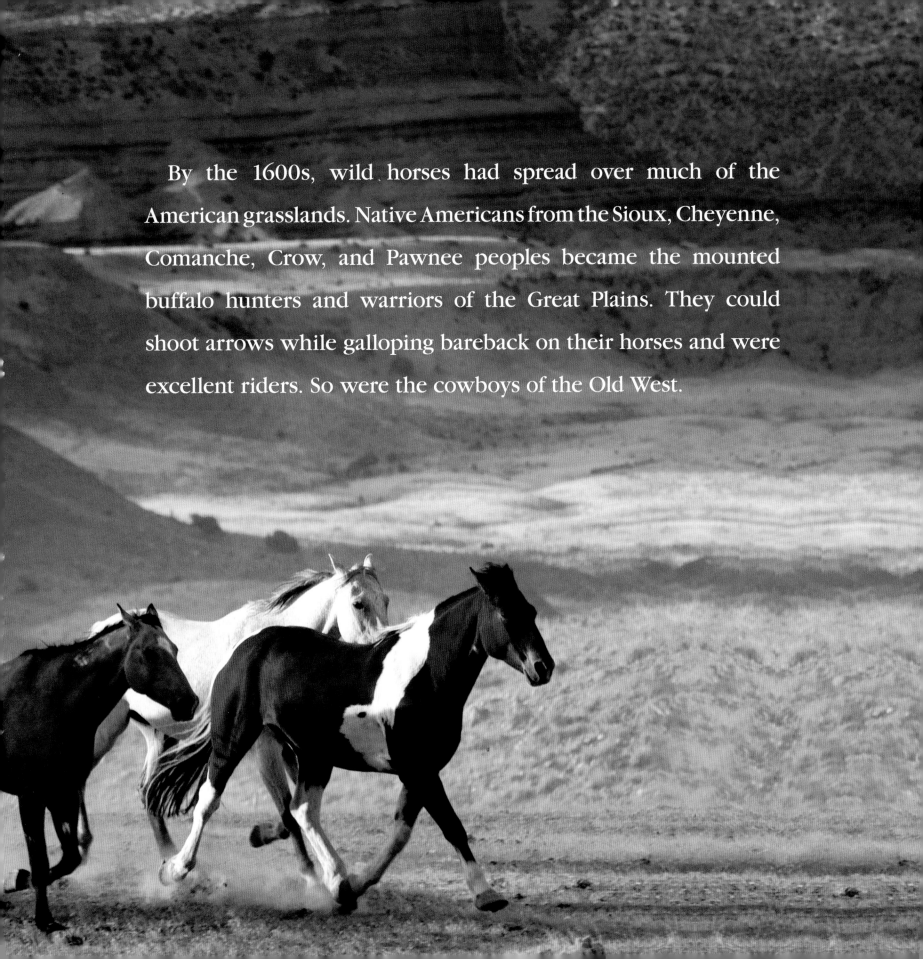

By the 1600s, wild horses had spread over much of the American grasslands. Native Americans from the Sioux, Cheyenne, Comanche, Crow, and Pawnee peoples became the mounted buffalo hunters and warriors of the Great Plains. They could shoot arrows while galloping bareback on their horses and were excellent riders. So were the cowboys of the Old West.

In the 1800s, horses were used to transport settlers traveling westward across America in wagon trains, groups of horse-drawn covered wagons called prairie schooners. For centuries, horses have played a vital role in American history.

For instance, modern industry would not have been possible without the use of horsepower. Before the invention of steam engines and gasoline engines, horses turned the wheels that provided power for machines in factories. This is how products such as cotton materials, flour, and iron were manufactured.

Today, machines mainly do the work that horses once did. But *horsepower* is still the term used to measure the pulling strength of a car, train, or plane engine. It seems that horses will always be with people in one way or another throughout time.

The most accurate way to tell a horse's age is by looking at its teeth and gums. This is why we use the expression "from the horse's mouth," which means "from the original source." It would not be a good idea for you to guess a horse's age by opening its mouth. Unless you're an expert, you may be bitten.

A horse's mouth is full of strong teeth used mostly for chewing and grinding grasses. Baby horses, called **foals**, have a full set of milk teeth when they are about nine months old, just like your baby teeth. Gradually the foals lose their milk teeth and grow permanent teeth. Over time, they wear down and change in shape and color and are then replaced by more teeth erupting from the jaw.

Horses rely heavily on their senses. They have larger eyes than most other animals. Since a horse's eyes are set on each side of its head, it can see in almost a complete circle and can look around while grazing. Horses can see some colors, such as yellow and green, but they cannot see all the colors you can see.

They can hear higher-pitched sounds than humans can. By moving their ears, they can pick up faint sounds that people cannot hear.

Horses can smell other animals and people up close and from far away. Smell is very important for horses. They recognize each other by their scent.

They can taste sweet foods. They love sugar or fruits, such as watermelon. Horses are also sensitive to touch. They can sense a fly landing anywhere on their bodies. Friendly horses often groom each other by nuzzling their **manes** and necks.

Horses don't talk of course, but they communicate in other ways. A horse moves its eyes and ears to show what it is feeling. When a horse lays back its ears and shows the whites of its eyes, it is angry or frightened. When the horse points its ears forward, it is interested in some object. When the horse lowers its ears, it is relaxed or sleeping. You can also tell that a horse is upset when it stamps a **hind leg**, shakes its head, and swishes its tail. Horses also make sounds such as **neighing**, nickering, and snorting. The sounds seem to show how the horse is feeling.

Male horses, known as **stallions**, try to show who is dominant (the leader) by fighting, **rearing**, and stabbing their front hooves or biting the neck of the other horse.

Horses can sense when people are frightened or angry, perhaps by their smell. Touching, patting, and grooming build trust between a human and a horse.

In spring or early summer, female horses, known as **mares**, mate with stallions. After about eleven months, a foal is born. Most births take place at night. When she is ready to give birth, the mare lies down. The foal usually is delivered in about fifteen minutes. A young mare is called a **filly**, and a young male is called a **colt**.

Right after the delivery, the mare gets up and licks her foal all over. In less than one hour, a foal is walking. It keeps in contact with its mother by bumping into her.

Horses move in four natural ways, called gaits or paces. They walk, trot, canter, and gallop. The walk is the slowest gait and the gallop is the fastest.

When a horse walks, each hoof leaves the ground at a different time. It moves one hind leg first, and then the front leg on the same side; then the other hind leg and the other front leg. When a horse walks, its body swings gently with each stride.

When a horse trots, its legs move in pairs, left front leg with right hind leg, and right front leg with left hind leg. When a horse canters, the hind legs and one front leg move together, and then the hind legs and the other foreleg move together.

The gallop is like a much faster walk, where each hoof hits the ground one after another. When a horse gallops, all four of its hooves may be flying off the ground at the same time.

Horses are usually described by their **coat** colors and by the white markings on their faces, bodies, legs, and hooves.

Some horses are all black, but most have at least a little brown in them. Bay horses range in color from dark to light brown, while chestnuts always have reddish coats. Palominos have a golden or yellow color. Roans and duns have pale gray or brown coats.

Partly colored horses are called pintos or paints. Colorless, pure-white horses—albinos—are rare. Most horses that look white are actually gray.

Skewbalds have brown and white patches. Piebalds have black-and-white patches. Spotteds have dark spots on a white coat or white spots on a dark coat.

Horses also vary in shape and size. Horses that look very much alike belong to the same breed. Just as spaniels, terriers, and collies are all still dogs, Arabians, Clydesdales, and mustangs are all still horses.

There are three groups of horse breeds—hotbloods, coldbloods, and warmbloods. Hotbloods originally came from the countries of North Africa and the Middle East, where the climate is hot. Coldbloods originally came from the countries of northern Europe, where the climate is cooler. A warmblood is the offspring of mating a hotblood and a coldblood.

Dating back more than forty-five hundred years, the Arabian is probably the oldest and best known of all the hotblood breeds. It is a small but tough horse.

Hundreds of years ago, Arabians were crossed with native English breeds to produce the type of hotblood called a Thoroughbred, the fastest and most expensive horse breed. Thoroughbreds are used in racing, steeplechasing, and other sports.

Coldblood breeds are large, heavy horses known for their calmness and patience. For centuries, Europeans used a particular coldblood breed to do farmwork and to pull heavy wagons.

The Shire is the biggest of the English coldbloods. It weighs as much as 2,200 pounds, more than the combined weight of all the students in your class. A pair of Shires is able to pull a load of fifty tons—about the weight of ten elephants.

Clydesdales are a bit smaller and lighter in weight than Shires. Clydesdales were used to plow the huge wheat fields and cornfields of the midwestern United States and central Canada.

Most of the horses we use today are warmbloods. Contest or sporting horses are developed specifically for riding or jumping in sports such as polo. In polo, players mounted on horses use a long-handled mallet to try to hit a ball through a goalpost. A polo pony is a horse that's fast and tough and can change direction quickly.

Ponies look different from horses. They are smaller, and they have short and usually hairy legs, sturdy bodies, and thick manes and tails.

The Dartmoor is a strong, tough pony that can carry a grown person. Some ponies live wild on the high open lands of Dartmoor, England. Their thick coats and shaggy manes and tails protect them in cold weather.

In the United States, there are many pony breeds, including the feral Chincoteague horses on Assateague, an island off the coast of Virginia; the Rocky Mountain; the Pony of the Americas; and the American Shetland, the most popular pony in the country. Today, there are about forty thousand Shetland ponies registered in the United States.

Horses' and ponies' heights are measured in *hands*, and each hand is equal to four inches. A pony is less than fourteen hands and two inches high, or fifty-eight inches.

At one time, most children who grew up on a farm or in the city learned how to care for a horse. Nowadays, few people ride horses, and even fewer own them.

Just like people, a horse needs to be given food, water, and shelter. It needs to be groomed, cleaned, and cared for. It needs regular exercise. In return, a horse can give us a wonderful feeling of close companionship and trust. And that's enough for true horse lovers.

GLOSSARY

Coat—The external growth on an animal.

Coldblood—Draft horses such as Clydesdales that have a calm nature and immense strength.

Colt—A young male horse usually less than four years in age.

Filly—A young female horse usually less than four years in age.

Foal—A young animal of the horse family less than one year in age.

Hands—A unit of length used to measure horses. One hand is equal to four inches.

Hind leg—The back limb of an animal with four limbs.

Hoof—A curved covering of horn that protects the front of or encloses the ends of the limbs of a horse.

Hotblood—Highly strung, temperamental horses such as racehorses that originally came from hotter countries in the world.

Mane—Long and heavy hair growing about the neck and head of some mammals.

Mare—A female horse of breeding age.

Neighing—Making the prolonged cry of a horse.

Rearing—A horse's rising up on its hind legs.

Shod—To place a horseshoe or similar protective plate on a horse's hoof.

Stallion—A male horse of breeding age.

Warmblood—The offspring of mating a hotblood and a coldblood. Horse types such as the palomino that have a mixture of temperaments. Often used for horseback riding, herding, and sporting events.

INDEX
Bold type indicates illustrations.

READ MORE ABOUT IT

Seymour Simon's website
www.seymoursimon.com

Equinespot
www.equinespot.com/
facts-about-horses.html

Learn About Horses
www.learn-about-horses.com